THE NEW COMPOSERS
Easy PIANO
VOLUME 2

**LUDOVICO EINAUDI • RACHEL PORTMAN • ENNIO MORRICONE
JOHN WILLIAMS • GIOVANNI ALLEVI • RICHARD CLAYDERMAN
HANS ZIMMER • JAMES HORNER • YANN TIERSEN • ALAN SILVESTRI
HOWARD SHORE • REMO ANZOVINO • ROBERTO CACCIAPAGLIA**

Piano arrangements
by Franco Concina

Volontè&Co

Foto in copertina: © iaremenko - Fotolia.com

© 2020 Volontè & Co. s.r.l. - Milano
All rights reserved.

CONTENTS

A GIFT OF A THISTLE /
FOR THE LOVE OF A PRINCESS *James Horner* 4

ARIA (PER RESPIRARE) *Giovanni Allevi* 18

BECOMING ONE OF "THE PEOPLE" /
BECOMING ONE WITH NEYTIRI *James Horner* 9

CONCERNING HOBBITS *Howard Shore* 28

HARRY'S WONDROUS WORLD *John Williams* 24

I'M FORREST... FORREST GUMP /
YOU'RE NO DIFFERENT *Alan Silvestri* 31

INDAGINE SU UN CITTADINO
AL DI SOPRA DI OGNI SOSPETTO *Ennio Morricone* 36

J'Y SUIS JAMAIS ALLÉ *Yann Tiersen* 39

LE ONDE *Ludovico Einaudi* 42

MARIAGE D'AMOUR *Paul de Senneville / Richard Clayderman* 48

NEFELI *Ludovico Einaudi* 60

NOW WE ARE FREE *Hans Zimmer, Klaus Badelt, Lisa Gerrard* 66

OCEANO *Roberto Cacciapaglia* 55

STAR WARS *John Williams* 70

STELLA DEL MATTINO *Ludovico Einaudi* 74

TABÙ *Remo Anzovino* 84

THE CIDER HOUSE RULES *Rachel Portman* 78

TIME *Hans Zimmer* 82

A GIFT OF A THISTLE / FOR THE LOVE OF A PRINCESS

(from *Braveheart*)

Music by James Horner

BECOMING ONE OF "THE PEOPLE" / BECOMING ONE WITH NEYTIRI

(from the Twentieth Century Fox Motion Picture AVATAR)

Music by James Horner

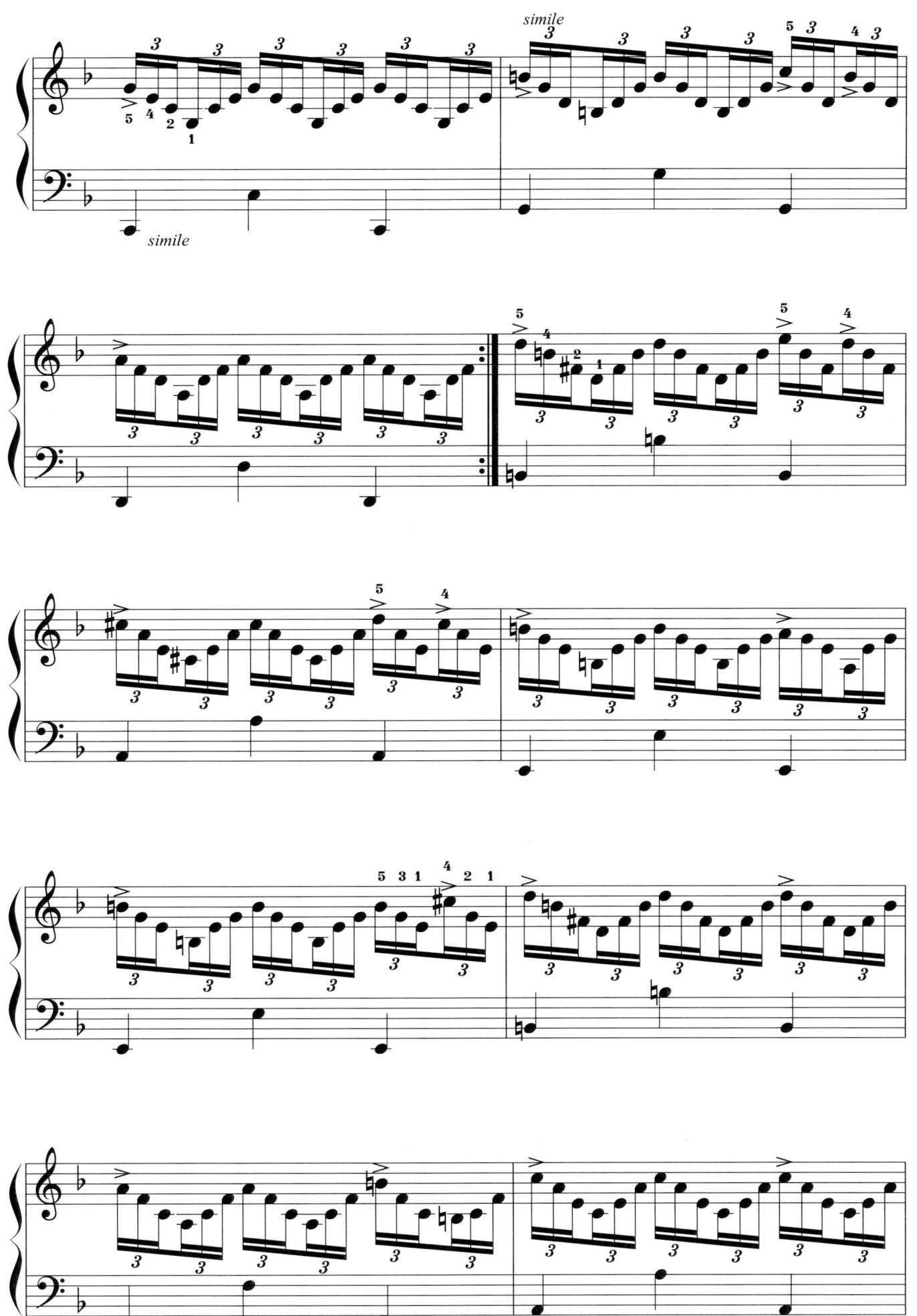

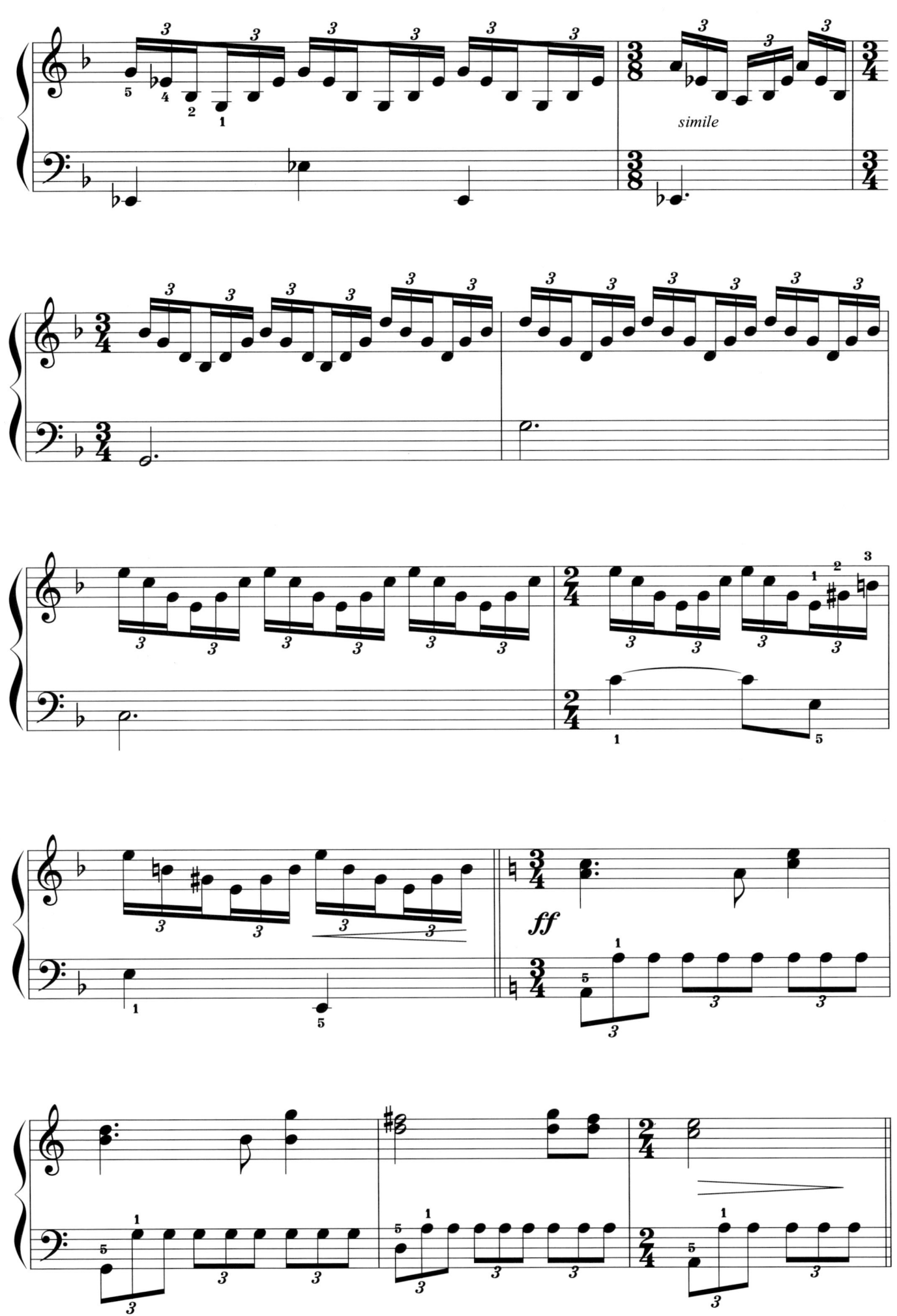

ARIA (PER RESPIRARE)

(from the Album *Allevilive* by Giovanni Allevi)

Music by Giovanni Allevi

HARRY'S WONDROUS WORLD

(from *Harry Potter and the Sorcerer's Stone*)

Music by John Williams

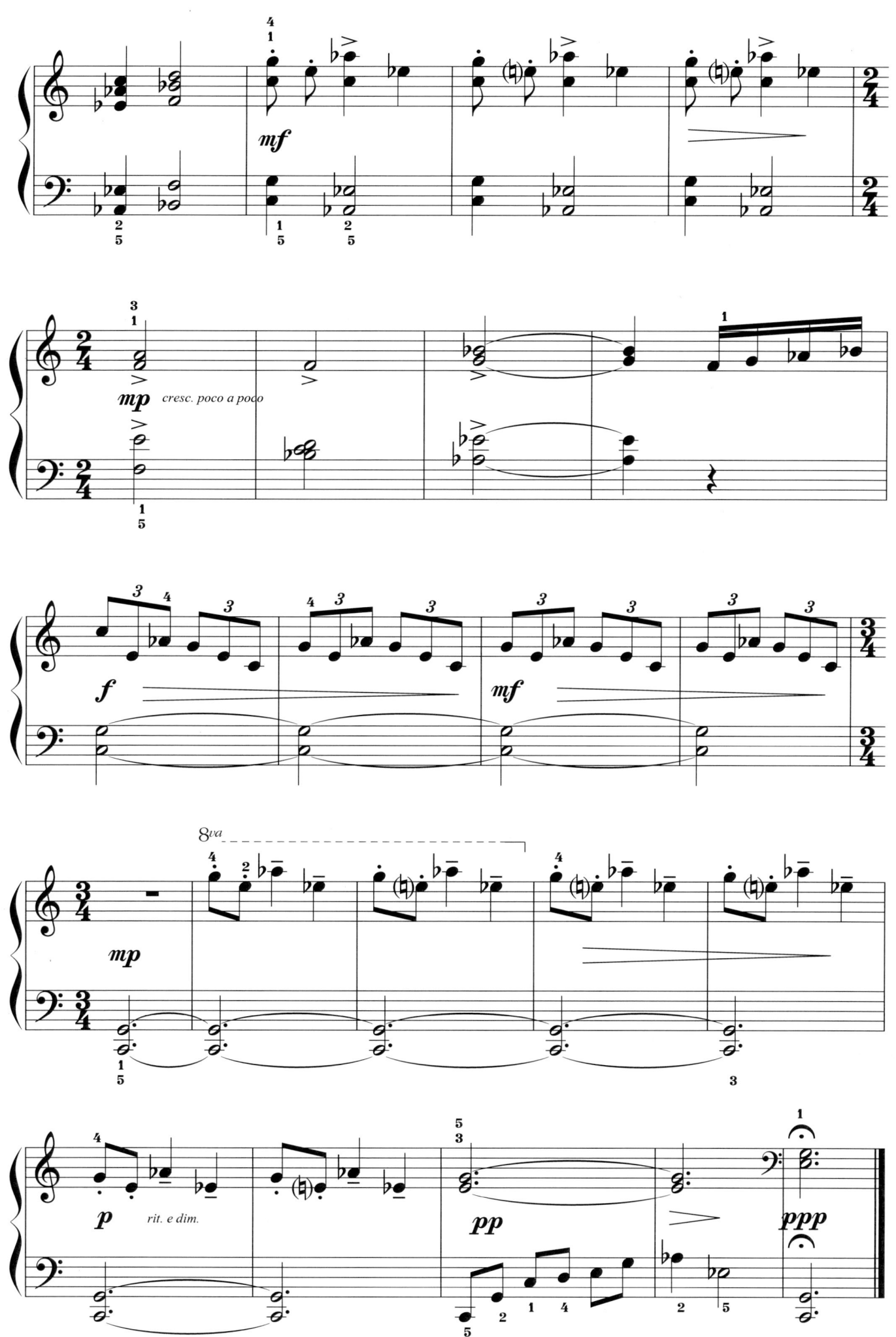

CONCERNING HOBBITS

(from *The Lord of the Rings: The Fellowship of the Ring*)

Music by Howard Shore

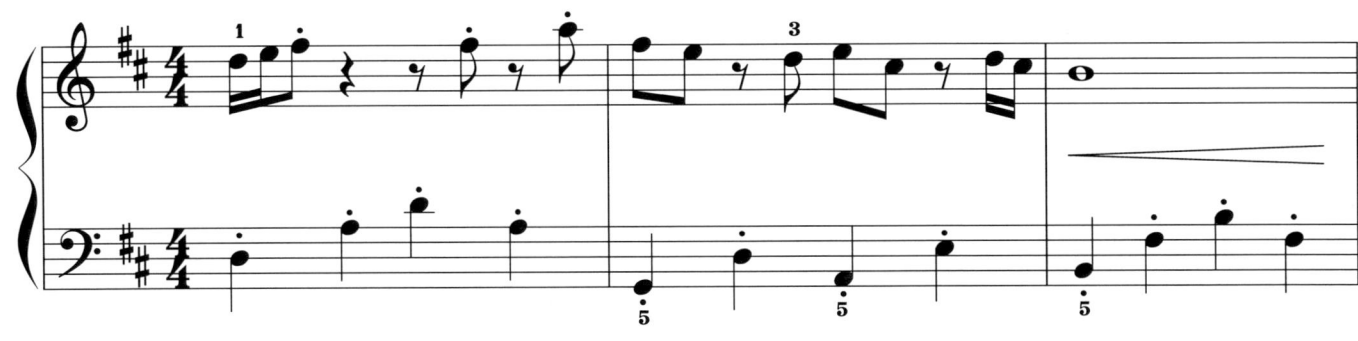

© 2001 NEW LINE TUNES (ASCAP)
All Rights (Excluding Print) Administered by UNIVERSAL MUSIC CORP. (ASCAP)
Exclusive Worldwide Print Rights Administered by ALFRED MUSIC
This Arrangement © 2019 NEW LINE TUNES (ASCAP)
All Rights Reserved. Used by Permission

I'M FORREST... FORREST GUMP / YOU'RE NO DIFFERENT

(from *Forrest Gump*)

Music by Alan Silvestri

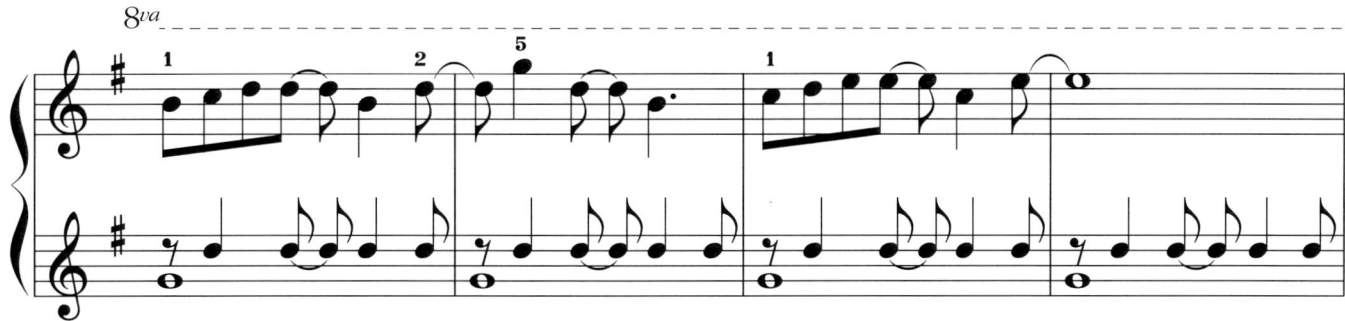

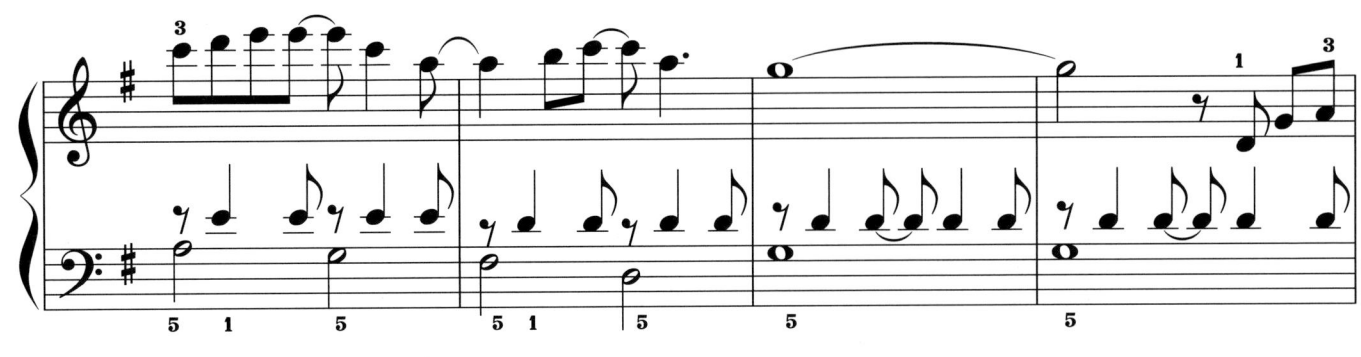

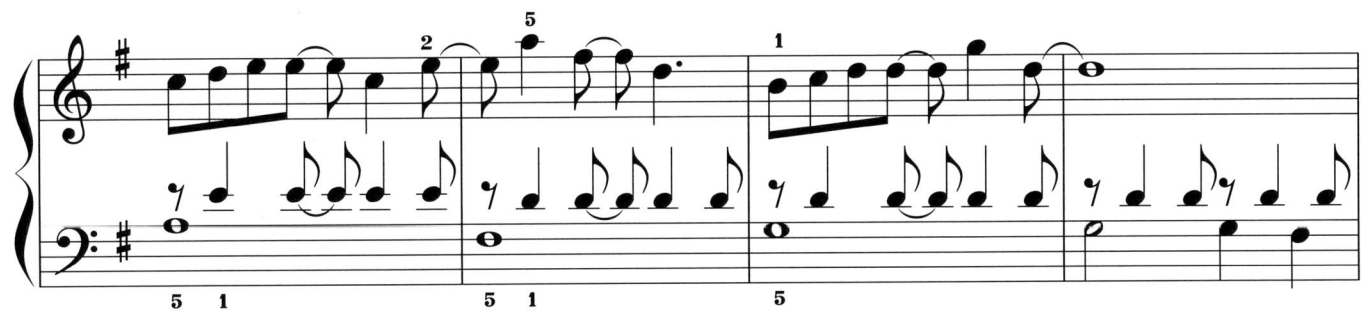
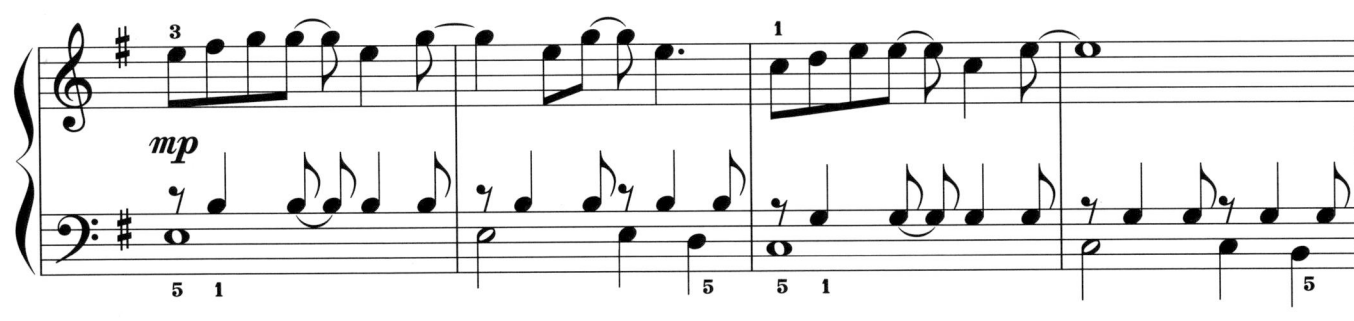
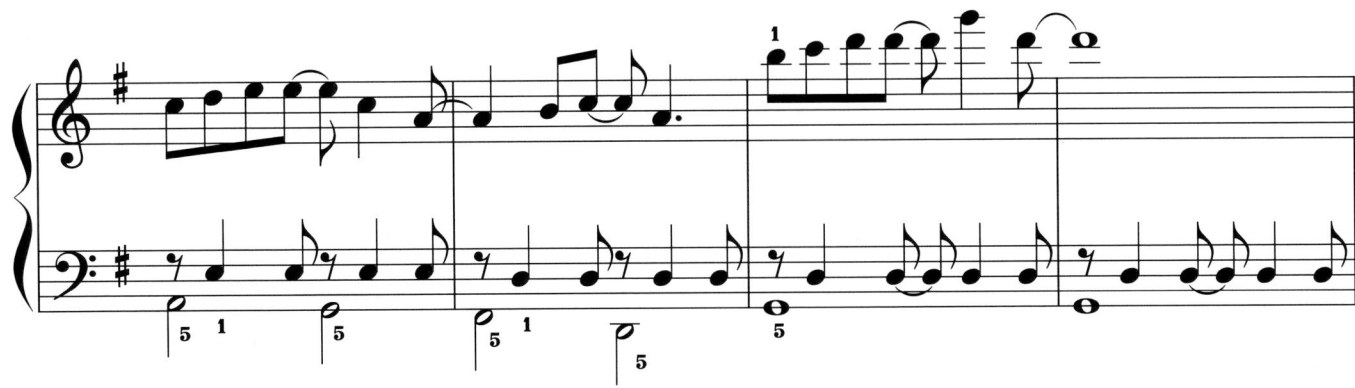

INDAGINE SU UN CITTADINO AL DI SOPRA DI OGNI SOSPETTO

(from *Indagine su un cittadino al di sopra di ogni sospetto*
a/k/a *Investigation of a Citizen Above Suspicion*)

Music by Ennio Morricone

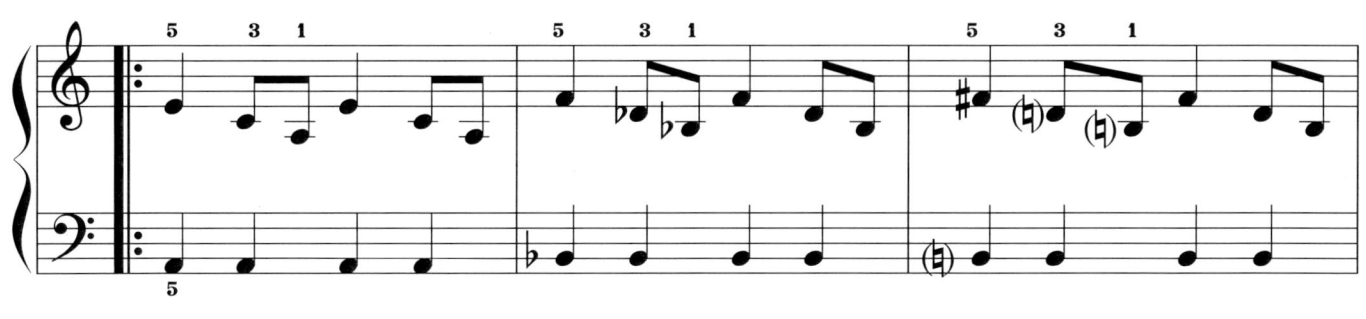
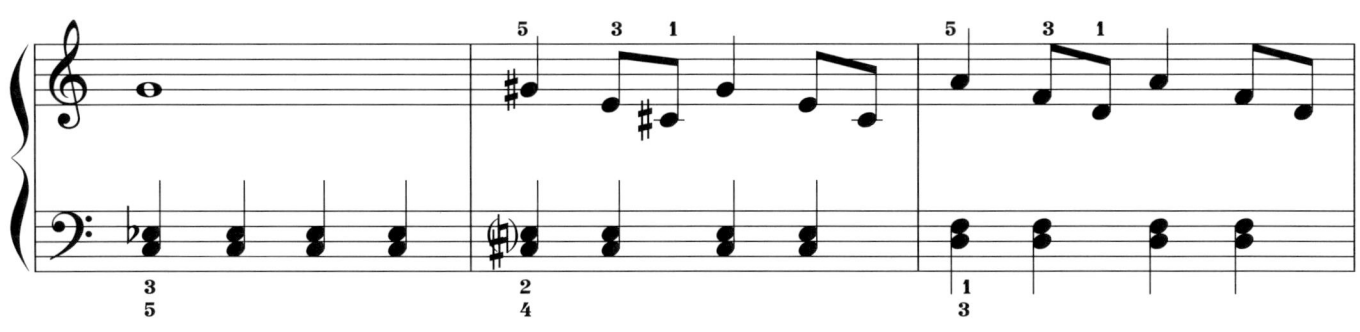
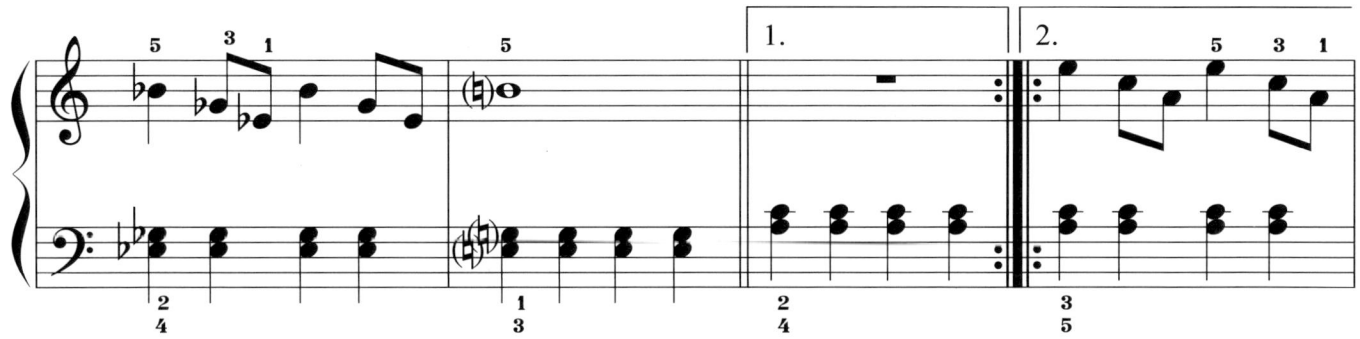
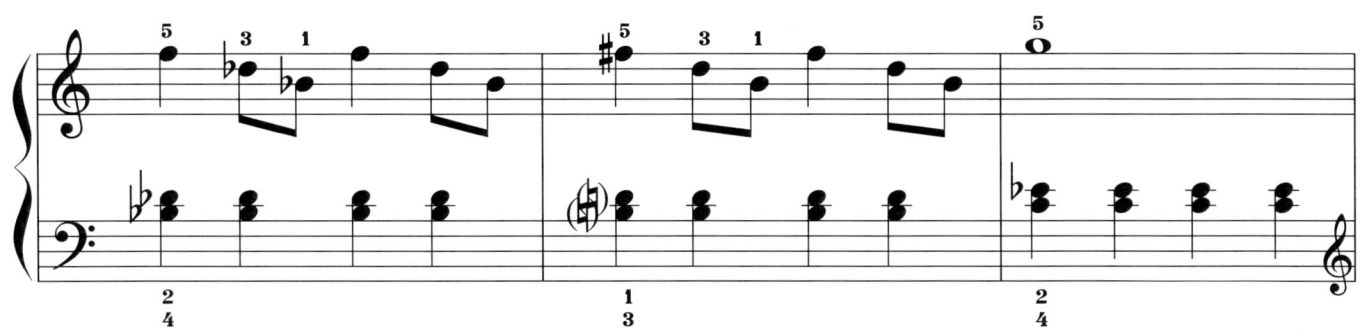
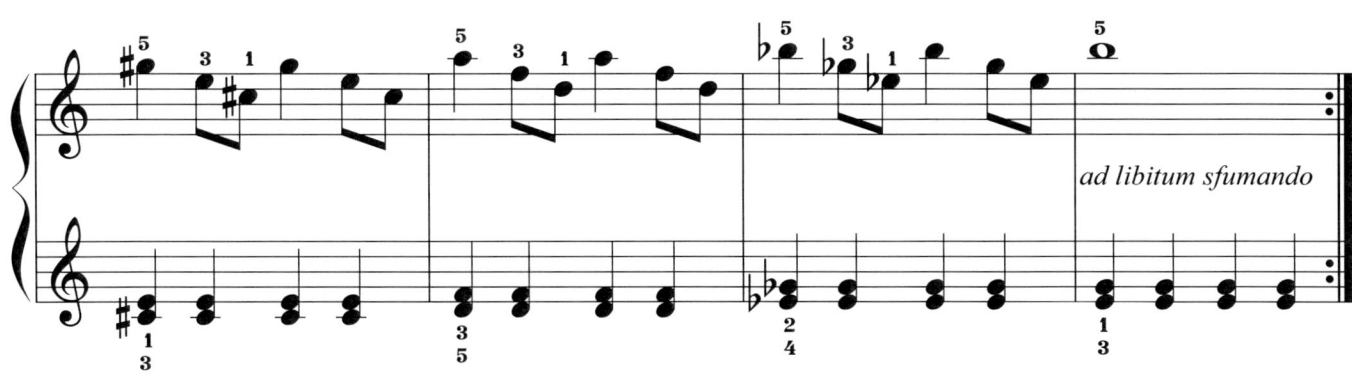

ad libitum sfumando

J'Y SUIS JAMAIS ALLÉ

(from the Album *Rue des Cascades* by Yann Tiersen
and *Le Fabuleux Destin d'Amélie Poulain* a/k/a *Amélie*)

Music by Yann Tiersen

Copyright © 1996 by Ici D'Ailleurs – Nancy, France / Universal Music Publishing MGB France – Paris, France
Sub-Publisher for Italy: Universal Music Publishing Ricordi S.r.l. – Via B. Crespi, 19 – 20159 Milano
All rights reserved. International Copyright secured
Reproduced by kind permission of Hal Leonard Europe S.r.l. – Italy

LE ONDE

(from the Album *Le Onde* by Ludovico Einaudi)

Music by Ludovico Einaudi

43

MARIAGE D'AMOUR

(from the Single *Lettre à Ma Mère* by Richard Clayderman)

Music by Paul M.A. de Senneville

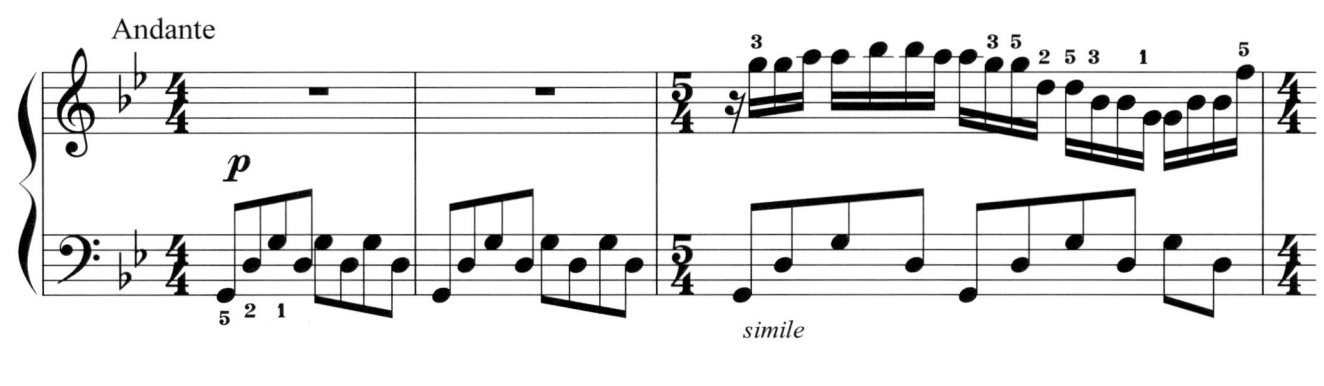
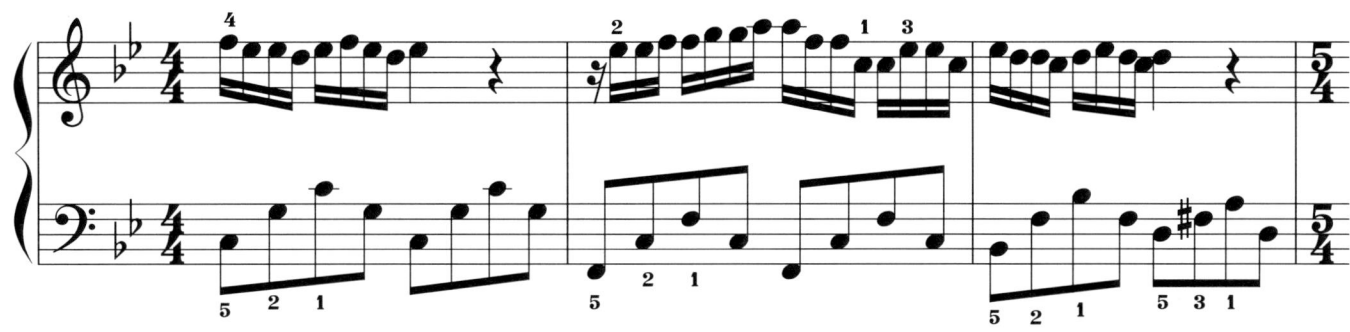
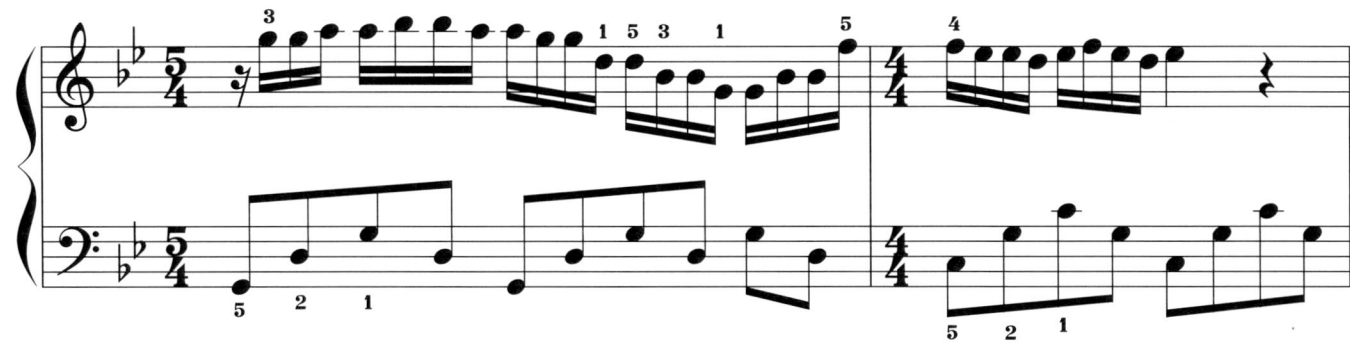
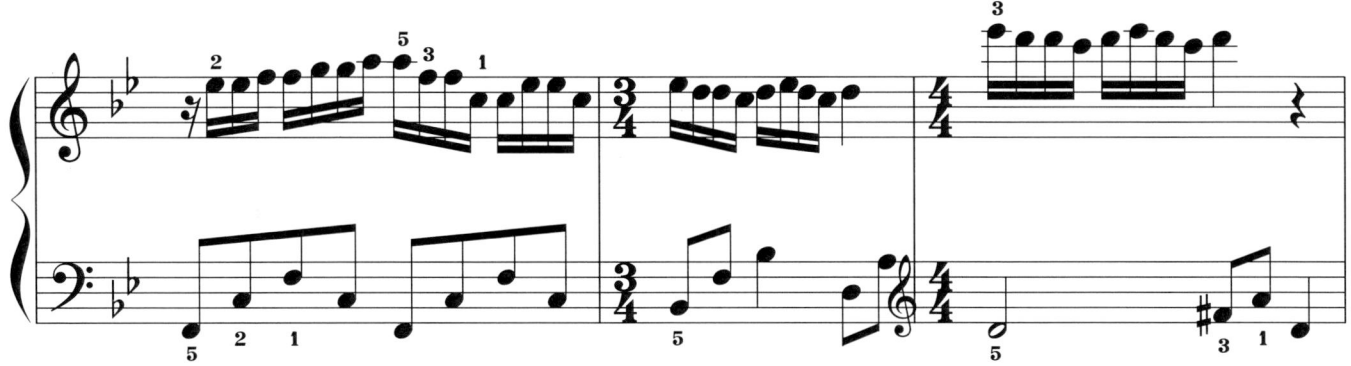

OCEANO

(from *Tree of Life – Expo Italy 2015*)

Music by Roberto Cacciapaglia

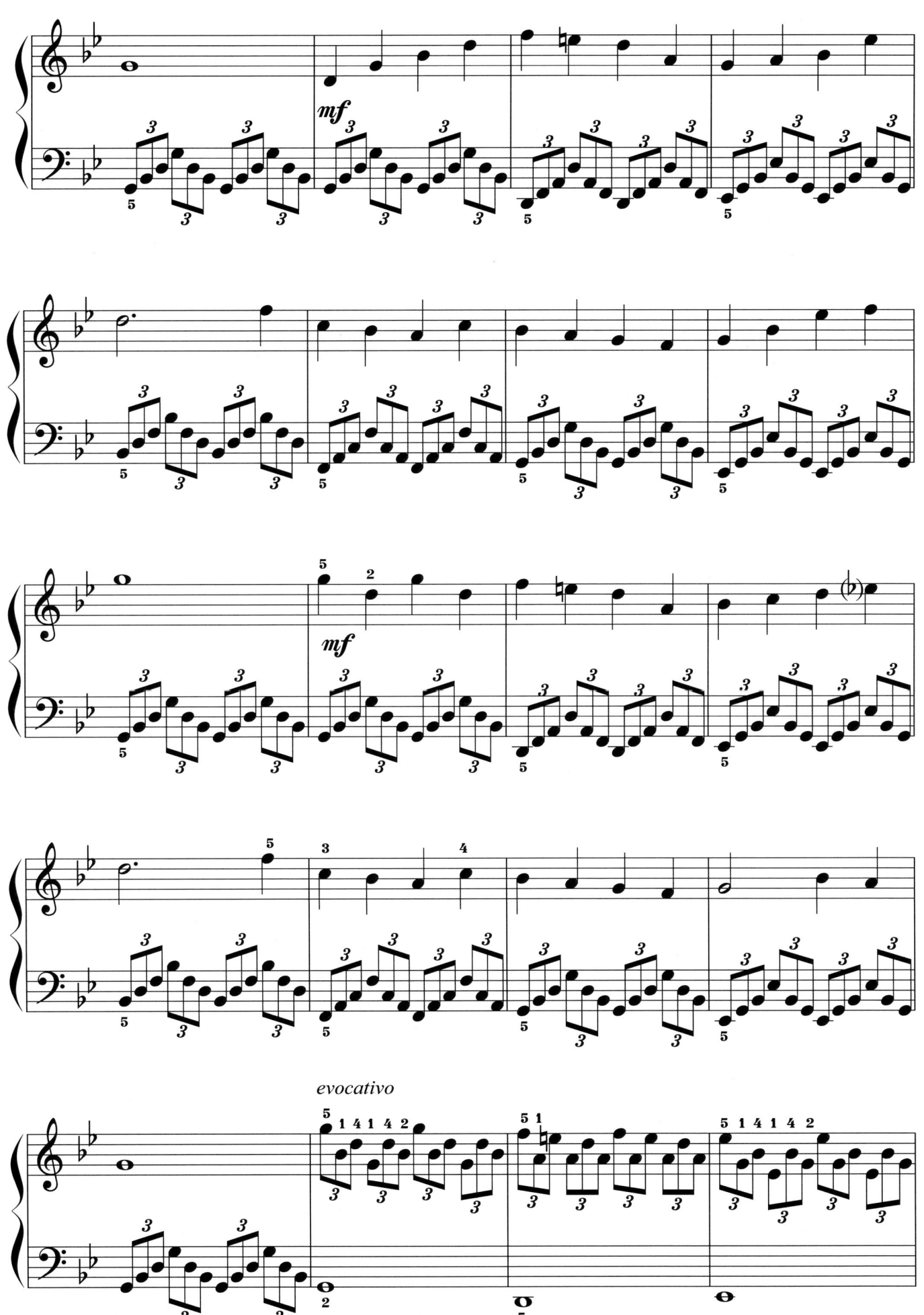

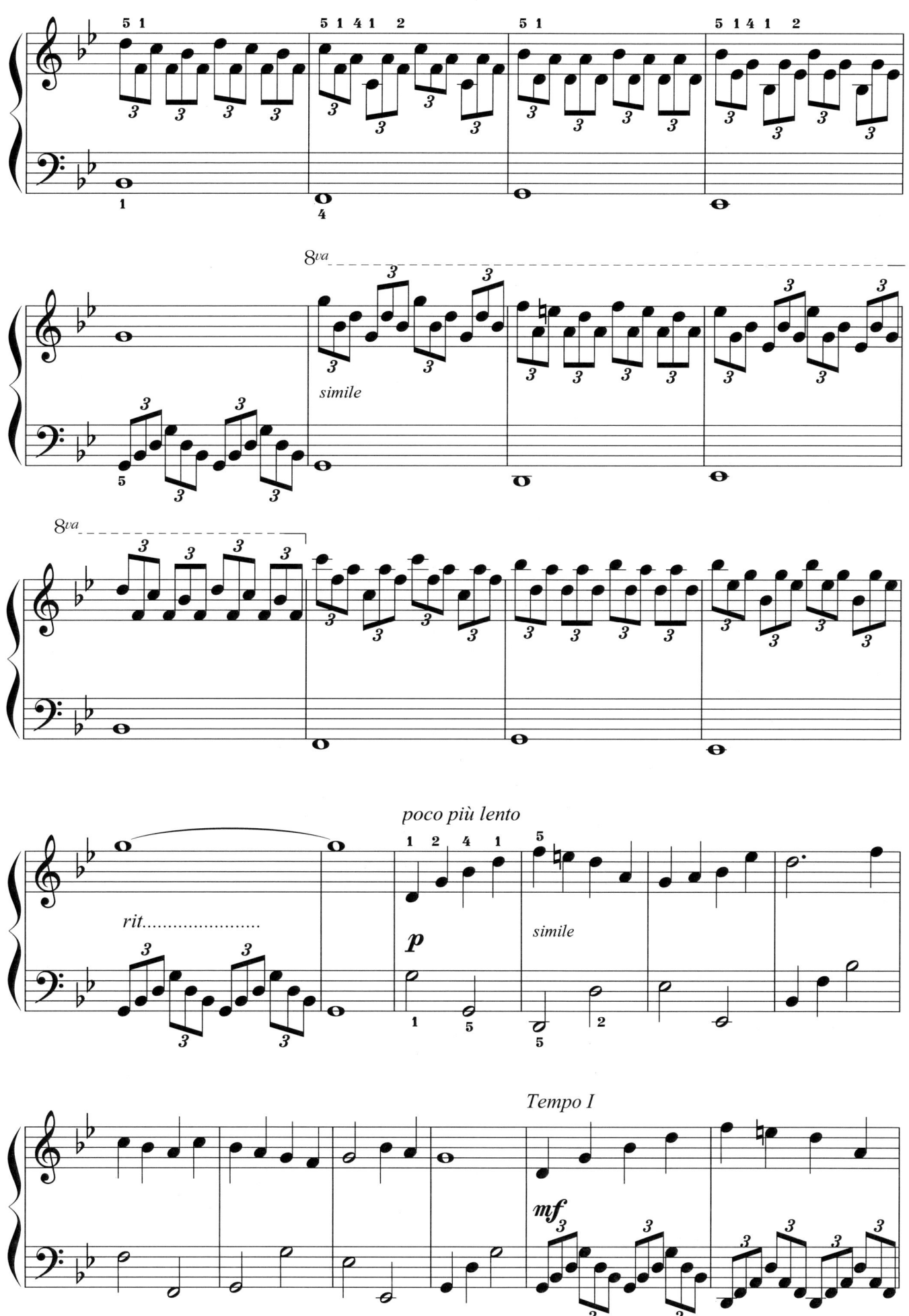

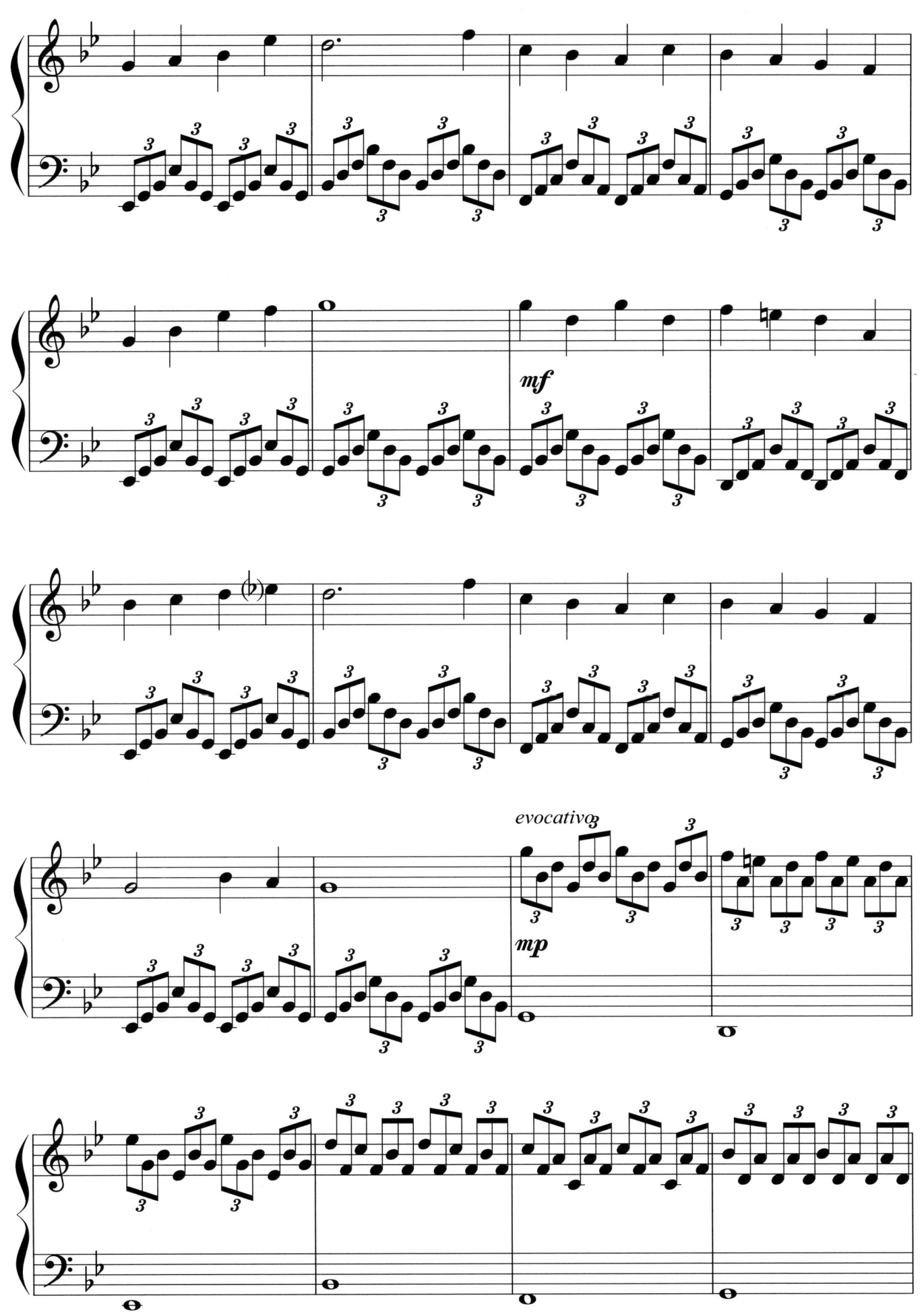

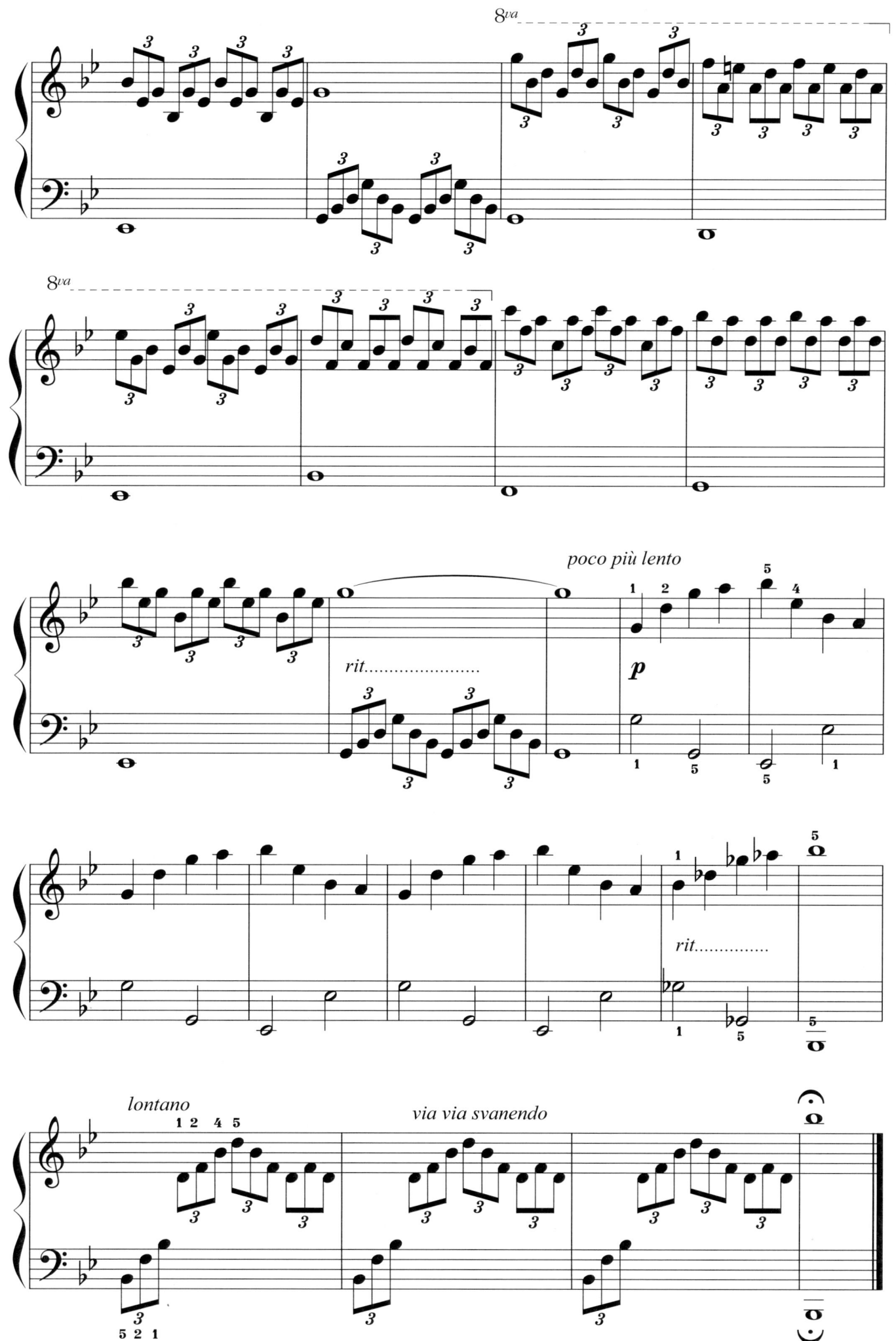

NEFELI

(from the Album *Eden Roc* by Ludovico Einaudi)

Music by Ludovico Einaudi

Andante con moto

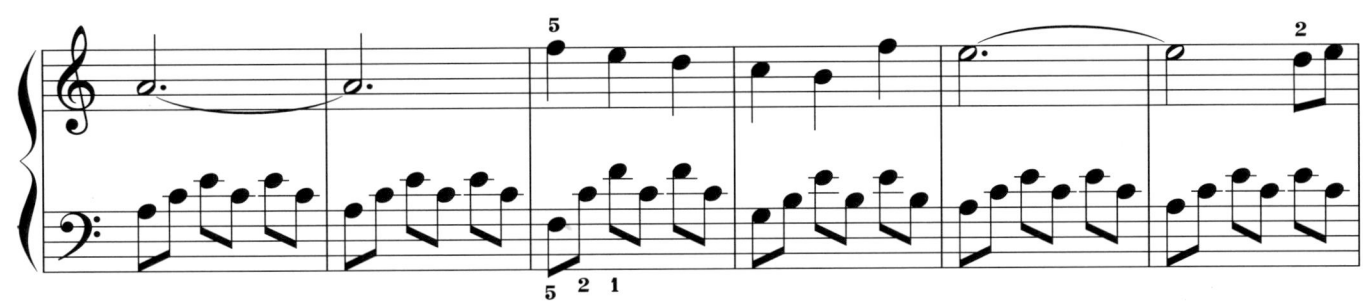

NOW WE ARE FREE
(from *Gladiator* Original Soundtrack)
Music by Klaus Badelt, Lisa G. Gerrard & Hans F. Zimmer

STAR WARS
(MAIN TITLE from Star Wars)

Music by John Williams

STELLA DEL MATTINO

(from the Album *I Giorni* by Ludovico Einaudi)

Music by Ludovico Einaudi

Andante con moto

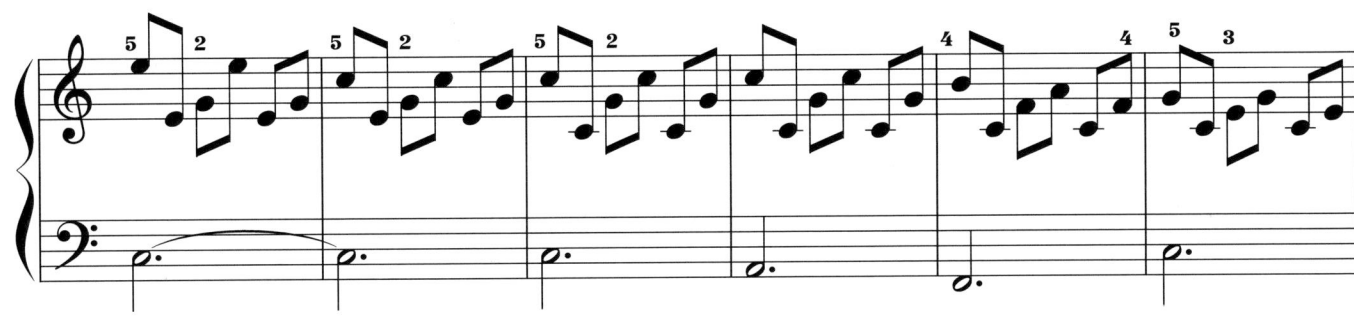

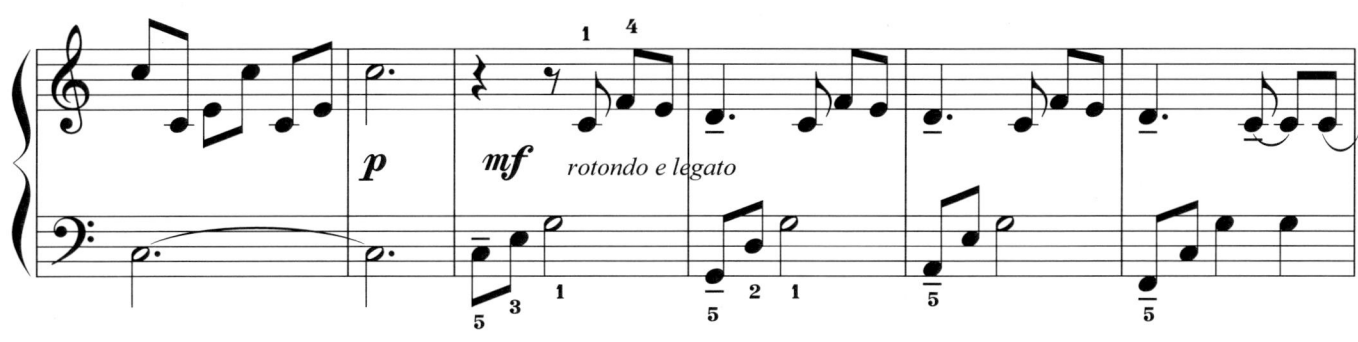

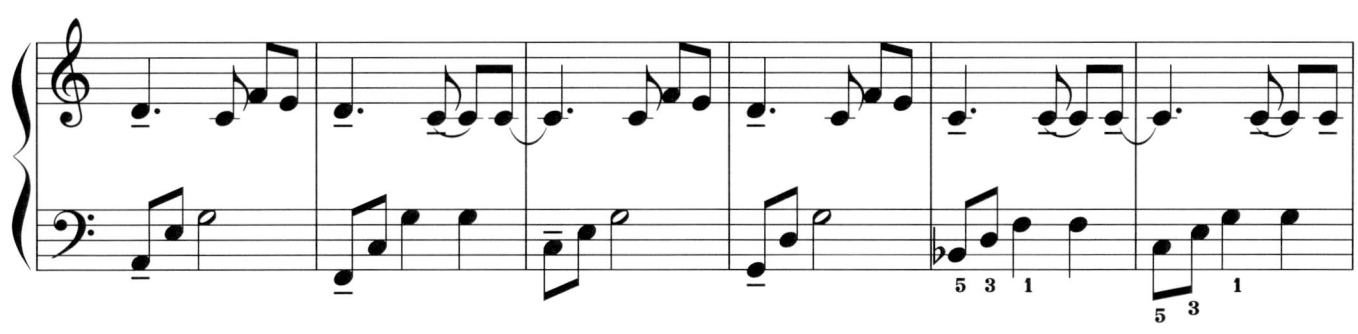
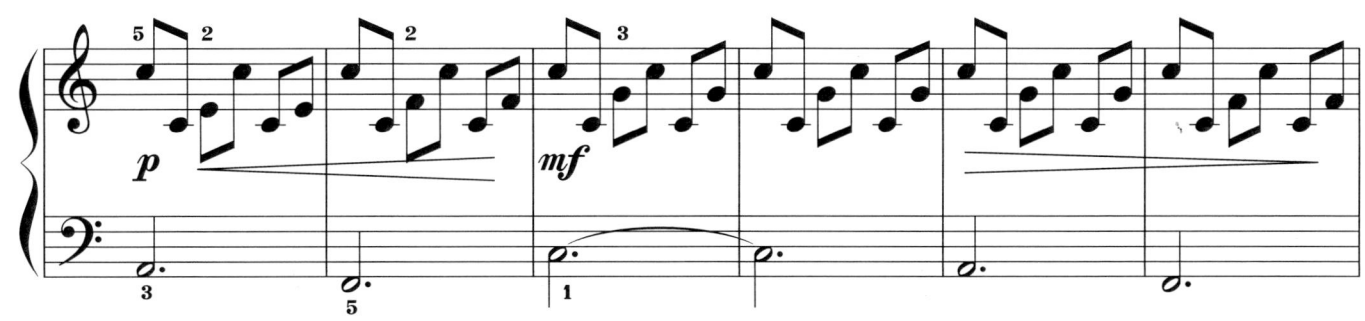

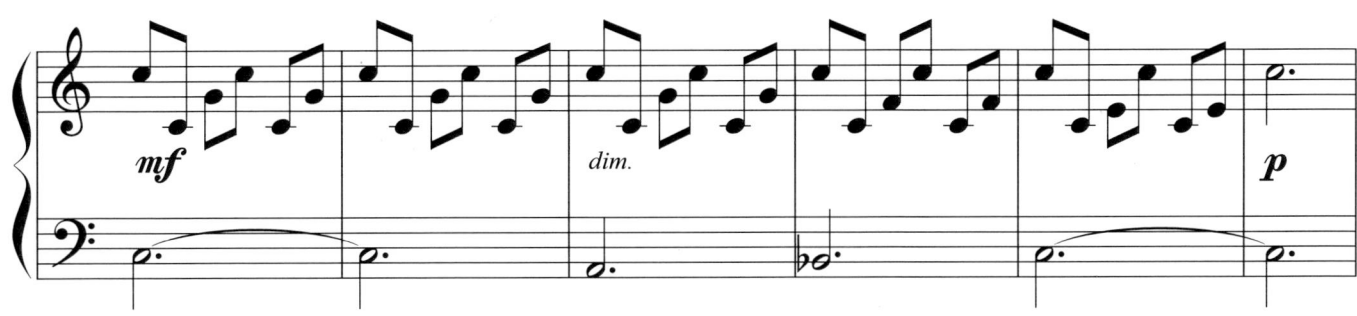
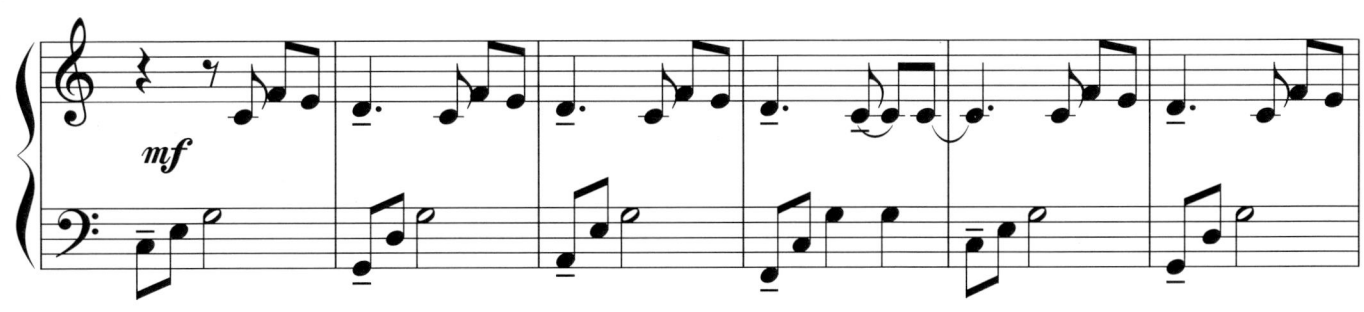

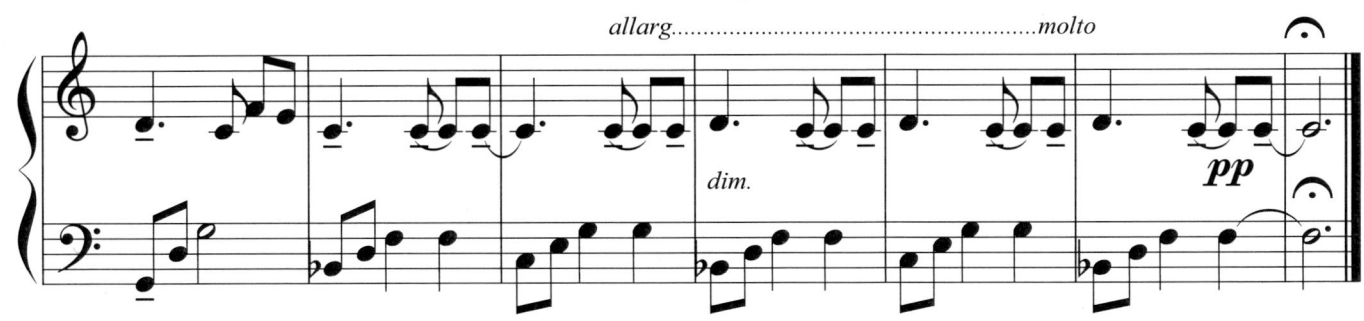

THE CIDER HOUSE RULES

(MAIN TITLE from *The Cider House Rules*)

Music by Rachel Portman

TIME

(from *Inception*)

Music by Hans Zimmer

TABÙ

(from the Album *Tabù* by Remo Anzovino)

Music by Remo Anzovino